AF813073

• SERIOUS FUN FOR GROWN UPS •

ndis

National Disability Insurance Scheme

Colour coded Invoice Tracker

GELATO

COLOURS EDITION

Also by the author :

Stardust
From Stardust
Stardust Alphabet
Stardust Numbers

More titles available soon.

This tracker has been designed by Kathryn Horton, an NDIS mum for other NDIS users in conjunction with Ten Twentyseven Publishing.

HOW TO USE

Welcome to the colour coded NDIS invoice tracker, a fun way to do not-so-fun tasks.

Customise the tracker to suit your needs by assigning colour sections by support worker, service providers such as occupational and speech therapists, month, or whatever works best for you.

A key page has been included for easy reference. Once you decide how you will use each colour section, write it in the matching colour box on the 'Key' page which will act as your index.

A medication page has been included to keep track of prescriptions and other important information for easy reference.

Happy tracking!

example

General

Ben – Monday and Tuesday

Eloise – Wednesday and Thursday

Alex– Friday

Consumables

Home Maintenance

Therapies

Ben

Ben : March 2025 –

[illegible]	[illegible]	[illegible]	[illegible]	[illegible]	[illegible]	[illegible]	[illegible]	[illegible]
10/3	0345	Social	5 hours	320.00	640.00	17/3	19/3	20/3
11/3	0345	Social	5 hours	320.00	640.00	17/3	19/3	20/3

Key

Wafer

Berry

Strawberry

Lemon

Blue Heaven

Pistachio

Peach

Contact Details

Support Worker Details

____

____

____

____

____

____

____

____

____

____

____

____

____

____

Important Information

PLAN DETAILS

Number ______________________________

Plan date ______________________________

Budget _________________________________

Budget breakdown ____________________

____

____

____

____

Goals ___________________________________

____

____

____

____

____

Medical Information

Specialists

SUPPORT DATE	INVOICE NUMBER	CATEGORY	DETAILS	CLAIM AMOUNT	INVOICE TOTAL	NDIS LODGEMENT DATE	NDIS PAYMENT RECIEVED DATE	DATE INVOICE PAID

SUPPORT DATE	INVOICE NUMBER	CATEGORY	DETAILS	CLAIM AMOUNT	INVOICE TOTAL	NDIS LODGEMENT DATE	NDIS PAYMENT RECIEVED DATE	DATE INVOICE PAID

SUPPORT DATE	INVOICE NUMBER	CATEGORY	DETAILS	CLAIM AMOUNT	INVOICE TOTAL	NDIS LODGEMENT DATE	NDIS PAYMENT RECIEVED DATE	DATE INVOICE PAID

SUPPORT DATE	INVOICE NUMBER	CATEGORY	DETAILS	CLAIM AMOUNT	INVOICE TOTAL	NDIS LODGEMENT DATE	NDIS PAYMENT RECIEVED DATE	DATE INVOICE PAID

SUPPORT DATE	INVOICE NUMBER	CATEGORY	DETAILS	CLAIM AMOUNT	INVOICE TOTAL	NDIS LODGEMENT DATE	NDIS PAYMENT RECIEVED DATE	DATE INVOICE PAID

SUPPORT DATE	INVOICE NUMBER	CATEGORY	DETAILS	CLAIM AMOUNT	INVOICE TOTAL	NDIS LODGEMENT DATE	NDIS PAYMENT RECIEVED DATE	DATE INVOICE PAID

SUPPORT DATE	INVOICE NUMBER	CATEGORY	DETAILS	CLAIM AMOUNT	INVOICE TOTAL	NDIS LODGEMENT DATE	NDIS PAYMENT RECIEVED DATE	DATE INVOICE PAID

SUPPORT DATE	INVOICE NUMBER	CATEGORY	DETAILS	CLAIM AMOUNT	INVOICE TOTAL	NDIS LODGEMENT DATE	NDIS PAYMENT RECIEVED DATE	DATE INVOICE PAID

SUPPORT DATE	INVOICE NUMBER	CATEGORY	DETAILS	CLAIM AMOUNT	INVOICE TOTAL	NDIS LODGEMENT DATE	NDIS PAYMENT RECIEVED DATE	DATE INVOICE PAID

SUPPORT DATE	INVOICE NUMBER	CATEGORY	DETAILS	CLAIM AMOUNT	INVOICE TOTAL	NDIS LODGEMENT DATE	NDIS PAYMENT RECIEVED DATE	DATE INVOICE PAID

SUPPORT DATE	INVOICE NUMBER	CATEGORY	DETAILS	CLAIM AMOUNT	INVOICE TOTAL	NDIS LODGEMENT DATE	NDIS PAYMENT RECIEVED DATE	DATE INVOICE PAID

SUPPORT DATE	INVOICE NUMBER	CATEGORY	DETAILS	CLAIM AMOUNT	INVOICE TOTAL	NDIS LODGEMENT DATE	NDIS PAYMENT RECIEVED DATE	DATE INVOICE PAID

SUPPORT DATE	INVOICE NUMBER	CATEGORY	DETAILS	CLAIM AMOUNT	INVOICE TOTAL	NDIS LODGEMENT DATE	NDIS PAYMENT RECIEVED DATE	DATE INVOICE PAID

SUPPORT DATE	INVOICE NUMBER	CATEGORY	DETAILS	CLAIM AMOUNT	INVOICE TOTAL	NDIS LODGEMENT DATE	NDIS PAYMENT RECIEVED DATE	DATE INVOICE PAID

SUPPORT DATE	INVOICE NUMBER	CATEGORY	DETAILS	CLAIM AMOUNT	INVOICE TOTAL	NDIS LODGEMENT DATE	NDIS PAYMENT RECIEVED DATE	DATE INVOICE PAID

SUPPORT DATE	INVOICE NUMBER	CATEGORY	DETAILS	CLAIM AMOUNT	INVOICE TOTAL	NDIS LODGEMENT DATE	NDIS PAYMENT RECIEVED DATE	DATE INVOICE PAID

SUPPORT DATE	INVOICE NUMBER	CATEGORY	DETAILS	CLAIM AMOUNT	INVOICE TOTAL	NDIS LODGEMENT DATE	NDIS PAYMENT RECIEVED DATE	DATE INVOICE PAID

SUPPORT DATE	INVOICE NUMBER	CATEGORY	DETAILS	CLAIM AMOUNT	INVOICE TOTAL	NDIS LODGEMENT DATE	NDIS PAYMENT RECIEVED DATE	DATE INVOICE PAID

SUPPORT DATE	INVOICE NUMBER	CATEGORY	DETAILS	CLAIM AMOUNT	INVOICE TOTAL	NDIS LODGEMENT DATE	NDIS PAYMENT RECIEVED DATE	DATE INVOICE PAID

SUPPORT DATE	INVOICE NUMBER	CATEGORY	DETAILS	CLAIM AMOUNT	INVOICE TOTAL	NDIS LODGEMENT DATE	NDIS PAYMENT RECIEVED DATE	DATE INVOICE PAID

SUPPORT DATE	INVOICE NUMBER	CATEGORY	DETAILS	CLAIM AMOUNT	INVOICE TOTAL	NDIS LODGEMENT DATE	NDIS PAYMENT RECIEVED DATE	DATE INVOICE PAID

SUPPORT DATE	INVOICE NUMBER	CATEGORY	DETAILS	CLAIM AMOUNT	INVOICE TOTAL	NDIS LODGEMENT DATE	NDIS PAYMENT RECIEVED DATE	DATE INVOICE PAID

SUPPORT DATE	INVOICE NUMBER	CATEGORY	DETAILS	CLAIM AMOUNT	INVOICE TOTAL	NDIS LODGEMENT DATE	NDIS PAYMENT RECIEVED DATE	DATE INVOICE PAID

SUPPORT DATE	INVOICE NUMBER	CATEGORY	DETAILS	CLAIM AMOUNT	INVOICE TOTAL	NDIS LODGEMENT DATE	NDIS PAYMENT RECIEVED DATE	DATE INVOICE PAID

SUPPORT DATE	INVOICE NUMBER	CATEGORY	DETAILS	CLAIM AMOUNT	INVOICE TOTAL	NDIS LODGEMENT DATE	NDIS PAYMENT RECIEVED DATE	DATE INVOICE PAID

SUPPORT DATE	INVOICE NUMBER	CATEGORY	DETAILS	CLAIM AMOUNT	INVOICE TOTAL	NDIS LODGEMENT DATE	NDIS PAYMENT RECIEVED DATE	DATE INVOICE PAID

SUPPORT DATE	INVOICE NUMBER	CATEGORY	DETAILS	CLAIM AMOUNT	INVOICE TOTAL	NDIS LODGEMENT DATE	NDIS PAYMENT RECIEVED DATE	DATE INVOICE PAID

SUPPORT DATE	INVOICE NUMBER	CATEGORY	DETAILS	CLAIM AMOUNT	INVOICE TOTAL	NDIS LODGEMENT DATE	NDIS PAYMENT RECIEVED DATE	DATE INVOICE PAID

SUPPORT DATE	INVOICE NUMBER	CATEGORY	DETAILS	CLAIM AMOUNT	INVOICE TOTAL	NDIS LODGEMENT DATE	NDIS PAYMENT RECIEVED DATE	DATE INVOICE PAID

SUPPORT DATE	INVOICE NUMBER	CATEGORY	DETAILS	CLAIM AMOUNT	INVOICE TOTAL	NDIS LODGEMENT DATE	NDIS PAYMENT RECIEVED DATE	DATE INVOICE PAID

SUPPORT DATE	INVOICE NUMBER	CATEGORY	DETAILS	CLAIM AMOUNT	INVOICE TOTAL	NDIS LODGEMENT DATE	NDIS PAYMENT RECIEVED DATE	DATE INVOICE PAID

SUPPORT DATE	INVOICE NUMBER	CATEGORY	DETAILS	CLAIM AMOUNT	INVOICE TOTAL	NDIS LODGEMENT DATE	NDIS PAYMENT RECIEVED DATE	DATE INVOICE PAID

SUPPORT DATE	INVOICE NUMBER	CATEGORY	DETAILS	CLAIM AMOUNT	INVOICE TOTAL	NDIS LODGEMENT DATE	NDIS PAYMENT RECIEVED DATE	DATE INVOICE PAID

SUPPORT DATE	INVOICE NUMBER	CATEGORY	DETAILS	CLAIM AMOUNT	INVOICE TOTAL	NDIS LODGEMENT DATE	NDIS PAYMENT RECIEVED DATE	DATE INVOICE PAID

SUPPORT DATE	INVOICE NUMBER	CATEGORY	DETAILS	CLAIM AMOUNT	INVOICE TOTAL	NDIS LODGEMENT DATE	NDIS PAYMENT RECIEVED DATE	DATE INVOICE PAID

SUPPORT DATE	INVOICE NUMBER	CATEGORY	DETAILS	CLAIM AMOUNT	INVOICE TOTAL	NDIS LODGEMENT DATE	NDIS PAYMENT RECIEVED DATE	DATE INVOICE PAID

SUPPORT DATE	INVOICE NUMBER	CATEGORY	DETAILS	CLAIM AMOUNT	INVOICE TOTAL	NDIS LODGEMENT DATE	NDIS PAYMENT RECIEVED DATE	DATE INVOICE PAID

SUPPORT DATE	INVOICE NUMBER	CATEGORY	DETAILS	CLAIM AMOUNT	INVOICE TOTAL	NDIS LODGEMENT DATE	NDIS PAYMENT RECIEVED DATE	DATE INVOICE PAID

SUPPORT DATE	INVOICE NUMBER	CATEGORY	DETAILS	CLAIM AMOUNT	INVOICE TOTAL	NDIS LODGEMENT DATE	NDIS PAYMENT RECIEVED DATE	DATE INVOICE PAID

SUPPORT DATE	INVOICE NUMBER	CATEGORY	DETAILS	CLAIM AMOUNT	INVOICE TOTAL	NDIS LODGEMENT DATE	NDIS PAYMENT RECIEVED DATE	DATE INVOICE PAID

SUPPORT DATE	INVOICE NUMBER	CATEGORY	DETAILS	CLAIM AMOUNT	INVOICE TOTAL	NDIS LODGEMENT DATE	NDIS PAYMENT RECIEVED DATE	DATE INVOICE PAID

SUPPORT DATE	INVOICE NUMBER	CATEGORY	DETAILS	CLAIM AMOUNT	INVOICE TOTAL	NDIS LODGEMENT DATE	NDIS PAYMENT RECIEVED DATE	DATE INVOICE PAID

SUPPORT DATE	INVOICE NUMBER	CATEGORY	DETAILS	CLAIM AMOUNT	INVOICE TOTAL	NDIS LODGEMENT DATE	NDIS PAYMENT RECIEVED DATE	DATE INVOICE PAID

SUPPORT DATE	INVOICE NUMBER	CATEGORY	DETAILS	CLAIM AMOUNT	INVOICE TOTAL	NDIS LODGEMENT DATE	NDIS PAYMENT RECIEVED DATE	DATE INVOICE PAID

SUPPORT DATE	INVOICE NUMBER	CATEGORY	DETAILS	CLAIM AMOUNT	INVOICE TOTAL	NDIS LODGEMENT DATE	NDIS PAYMENT RECIEVED DATE	DATE INVOICE PAID

SUPPORT DATE	INVOICE NUMBER	CATEGORY	DETAILS	CLAIM AMOUNT	INVOICE TOTAL	NDIS LODGEMENT DATE	NDIS PAYMENT RECIEVED DATE	DATE INVOICE PAID

SUPPORT DATE	INVOICE NUMBER	CATEGORY	DETAILS	CLAIM AMOUNT	INVOICE TOTAL	NDIS LODGEMENT DATE	NDIS PAYMENT RECIEVED DATE	DATE INVOICE PAID

SUPPORT DATE	INVOICE NUMBER	CATEGORY	DETAILS	CLAIM AMOUNT	INVOICE TOTAL	NDIS LODGEMENT DATE	NDIS PAYMENT RECIEVED DATE	DATE INVOICE PAID

Made in United States
Orlando, FL
06 November 2026

90230143R00045